Ancient Greek Gods and Their Powers

Children's Ancient History Books

BABY PROFESSOR

EDUCATION KIDS

Speedy Publishing LLC
40 E. Main St. #1156
Newark, DE 19711
www.speedypublishing.com

The Ancient Greeks believed in many gods. Each god had different powers.

Greek mythology
has twelve main
goddesses and gods.

They rule from
Mount Olympus
in Greece.

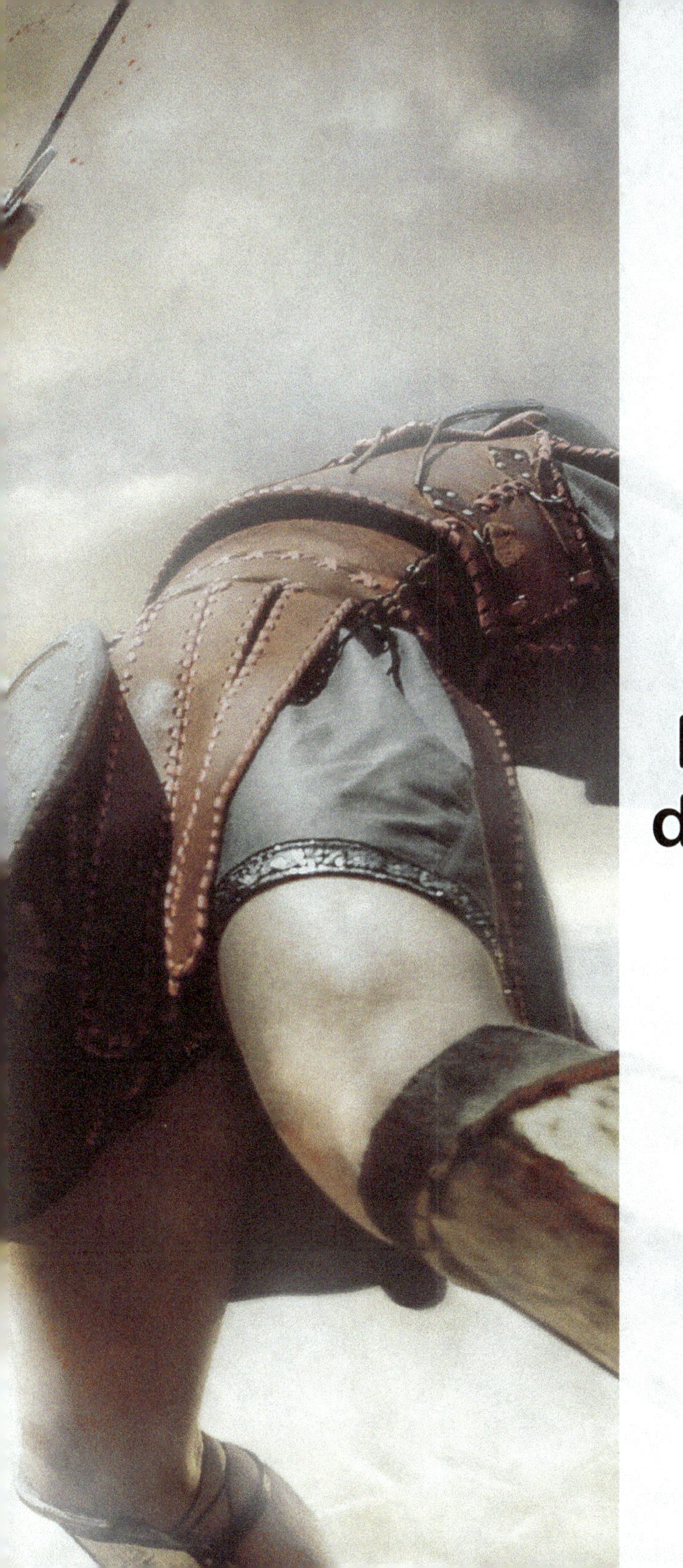

These gods
and goddesses
obtained their
power when Zeus
defeated his father,
Kronos, who
was the leader
of the Titans.

Let's get to know each of these gods and goddesses.

Zeus – the most powerful. His emotions affect the weather. When he is not happy, there will be thunderbolts.

Hera – is known as the marriage goddess and she is the wife of Zeus. She can bless or curse a marriage. She helps protect women from rape and dangers during childbirth.

Poseidon – is the sea god. He is considered as most powerful after Zeus, who is his brother. When he is not happy, he can cause earthquakes.

Hades – is the king of those who have died. He rules the underworld. He can control the dead and the riches of the world such precious stones and metals. He is also a brother of Zeus. He kidnapped and married Demeter's daughter named Persephone.

Aphrodite – is the goddess of beauty and love. She protects sailors. She can transform ordinary things and people through love. She could be daughter of Zeus and Dione. But there are also those who believe that she was born from a sea shell.

Apollo – is the god of healing and music. He can heal, but can also send plagues and illnesses. He is an archer and uses a silver bow to hunt. He is the son of the Titan Leto and Zeus.

Ares– is the war god.
He is powerful and
cruel. He is son of Hera
and Zeus. But because
he is mischievous, his
parents don't like him.

Artemis – protects women during the time they bear their children. She can either heal or inflict pain through plagues. She is the goddess of hunting and uses her silver arrows to hunt. She is Apollo's twin.

Athena – is the wisdom goddess. She has authority over wisdom and crafts. She is very skillful in war and she helps heroes like Odysseus, Hercules, and many others. She sprang out of Zeus' forehead and is his favorite child.

Hephaestus – is the god of the forge and fire. Even though he makes weapons and armor for the gods, he definitely loves peace. He is the son of Hera and Zeus. Aphrodite is his wife.

Hestia – is the goddess of the hearth, which means the fireplace and, by extension, the home. She is considered as the most gentle among all the gods. She is an older sister of Zeus. She is the oldest Olympian.

Hermes – is the god of messages, a friend of thieves, and loves to trick people. He is believed to have founded the sports known as gymnastics and boxing. He can give luck and wealth. He is the son of Maia and Zeus. He is the fastest of all the gods and he wears sandals and a hat that have wings. He carries a magic wand.

Demeter – is the fertility and wine goddess. She was the one who was believed to have invented wine. She can give a bountiful harvest. She is the child of Zeus and a mortal woman named Semele.

There are more interesting facts and stories about the Ancient Greek gods. Research and have fun!

Visit
BABY PROFESSOR
EDUCATION KIDS
www.BabyProfessorBooks.com
to download Free Baby Professor eBooks
and view our catalog of new and exciting
Children's Books